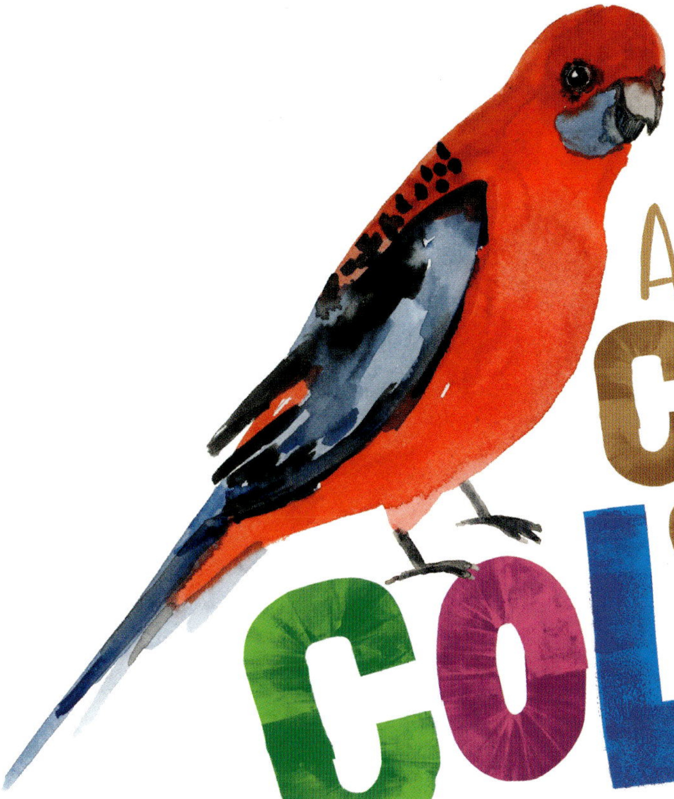

Australia: COUNTRY OF COLOUR

JESS RACKLYEFT

This is a COUNTRY OF COLOUR

Australia is the home of vivid red dirt, big blue skies, wild green bushland and warm golden beaches. This very large island has allowed unique, colourful and incredible plants and animals to adapt and grow, many of which can't be found anywhere else in the world.

Inspired by its bright and pure light, many poets and artists have celebrated Australia's striking colours over the years. In the early 20th century, a young and homesick Australian named Dorothea Mackellar wrote her famous poem, 'My Country'. In it, she wrote:

I love a sunburnt country,
A land of sweeping plains,
Of ragged mountain ranges,
Of droughts and flooding rains.
I love her far horizons,
I love her jewel-sea,
Her beauty and her terror –
The wide brown land for me!

A stark white ring-barked forest
All tragic to the moon,
The sapphire-misted mountains,
The hot gold hush of noon.
Green tangle of the brushes,
Where lithe lianas coil,
And orchids deck the tree-tops
And ferns the warm dark soil.

In this book, you will find an ode to many of these colours, in words and paint, from bright blue butterflies to electric yellow Billy Buttons *(Craspedia variabilis)*.

Colour is all around us. You might like to find your own colours in the wild and create a painted rainbow of what you see! Perhaps you might like to write about the colours, just like Dorothea did. Looking out for colour in your world can help you find things you may have never noticed before. Above all else, by immersing yourself in nature's paintbox you will appreciate this rainbow of life around you in new and exciting ways.

SEEING COLOUR

Looking at colour deeply is one of my favourite ways to explore new places. I grew up around the sand dunes of Western Australia as a kid – a stark, windy place of white hills leading down to an endless line of bright blue sea. When we holidayed, I always loved looking at the different colours in these new environments. When I think about the places I've been, colour is my first memory! I recall brushing the vibrant red dirt of Meekatharra off my hands, looking up at the lush green leaves of the Daintree, diving into the bright aquas of the Esperance sea and watching a vivid pink dawn at Byron Bay.

As an illustrator, I am still always thinking about colour. I like to look and wonder at the world around me, and I gather inspiration from nature. I live near a creek and I love seeing the shimmer of gold in the early morning mist there and quietly watching the tiny orange and brown Eastern Spinebills (*Acanthorhynchus tenuirostris*) darting about the riverbank. At home in my garden, I love spotting the green shine of a beetle's back among the grass and seeing the sky's purple glow just after the sun goes down.

FEELING COLOUR

Colours can affect how we feel. I find painting blue to be very calming, and when I create big artworks using green, I feel like I am in a forest! Here are some other ways that colour can make us feel:

RED
Strong emotions like love, passion and anger – 'seeing red!'

ORANGE
Courage, happiness and enthusiasm.

YELLOW
Uplifting, warming and joyful.

GREEN
Nature, growth and jealousy – 'green with envy'.

BLUE
Peaceful, trusting and calming. It can also represent sadness or 'feeling blue'.

VIOLET
Spiritual, brave and creative.

You might get a different mood from certain colours or see different colours in the world around you. Perhaps you might like to make a diary when you travel and create some art with the colours of the places you visit? Australia is home to many unique and colourful places, plants and animals.

Let's take a closer look at the world around us in this incredible country of colour!

RED + PINK

ULUṞU

The lands of the Yankunytjatjara and Pitjantjatjara people, Aṉangu land.

Uluṟu is found in the ‘Red Centre’ or ‘red heart’ of Australia, within the World Heritage-listed Uluṟu-Kata Tjuṯa National Park.

The vivid red colour of Uluṟu is created from the rusting of iron, found naturally in the rock. Like an iceberg, what we see is only the tip – Uluṟu continues more than 2.5 kilometres underground.

Red and pink are powerful colours in nature – they stand out and grab your attention! This works in the favour of plants that need to be pollinated because they attract hungry insects and birds with their bright flowers. Scientists have found that red can provide a warning, like the fiery back of a Redback Spider (*Latrodectus hasselti*). In art, red is described as a warming, powerful colour, and it can symbolise both danger and love. I love the dramatic names of some of my red and pink paints: crimson, vermilion, coral and ruby red.

Red-Eyed Tree Frog

(Litoria chloris)

Found in rainforest trees, these frogs have a distinctive call – a long moan followed by a soft trill.

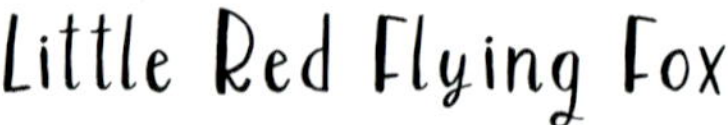

Little Red Flying Fox

(Pteropus scapulatus)

These clever bats can drink water by gathering it onto their fur from streams while they fly!

Redback Spider

(Latrodectus hasselti)

Only the female spiders have the famous red back and painful, venomous bite. Male redbacks live for several months, while females can live for 2–3 years.

Crimson Rosella

(Platycercus elegans)

The eye-catching Crimson Rosella is a vibrant red, but its relatives can be found in other colours, such as the Yellow Rosella, located on the Murray River.

Brogo Overflow

(Callistemon subulatus)

In summer, these flower spikes grow to around the size of your hand.

Giant Gippsland Earthworm

(Megascolides australis)

These long worms can grow up to 3 m and are found underground by the sucking noise they make when moving about.

Christmas Island Red Crab

(Gecarcoidea natalis)

Every year, millions of these crabs migrate from the forest to the beach, creating quite a spectacle. There are estimated to be 45 million of them on Christmas Island!

Common Heath

(Epacris impressa)

A sweet treat for nectar-eating birds, this plant is also the floral state emblem for Victoria.

Red-Bellied Black Snake

(Pseudechis porphyriacus)

These highly venomous snakes can submerge underwater to hide or lie on the rippling surface while looking a bit like a stick!

Major Mitchell's Cockatoo

(Lophochroa leadbeateri)

These birds mate for life and share parenting duties, like keeping eggs warm in their tree-hollow nest.

Lined Firetail Skink

(Morethia ruficauda)

A little lizard, laying only 1–3 eggs each clutch. Scientists think it may communicate by waving its bright tail!

Tasmanian Waratah

(Telopea truncata)

Each big flower is actually a cluster of smaller flowers and seedpods that look like tiny bananas!

Little Red Kaluta

(Dasykaluta rosamondae)

Found in the deserts of north-western Australia, these tiny marsupials escape the heat in summer by foraging at night. In winter, they forage during the day.

Scarlet Banksia

(Banksia coccinea)

These tall (up to 8 m) plants grow in sandy soil. After bushfires, the plant releases seeds for regeneration.

Crimson Chat

(Epthianura tricolor)

When drought hits inland, the Crimson Chat will travel towards the ocean in search of wetter environments.

Royal Grevillea

(Grevillea victoriae)

The striking flowers are a favourite snack for birds like the Eastern Spinebill *(Acanthorhynchus tenuirostris)* and Yellow-Faced Honeyeater *(Caligavis chrysops)*.

Pigface

(Carpobrotus glaucescens)

A sand dune-friendly plant growing by the sea, Pigface can survive in poor soils and full sun. It has edible fruit and leaves.

Flame Bottletree

(Brachychiton acerifolius)

Also known as the Illawarra Flame Tree. In spring and summer, this spectacular tree is covered in flame red bell-shaped flowers.

Scarlet Honeyeater

(Myzomela sanguinolenta)

The smallest honeyeater in Australia! These birds build tiny delicate nests made of spiderwebs and bark.

Small-Headed Blind Snake

(Anilios affinis)

There are many species of Blind Snakes and they are often mistaken for big earthworms. They have smooth scales so they can glide through soil.

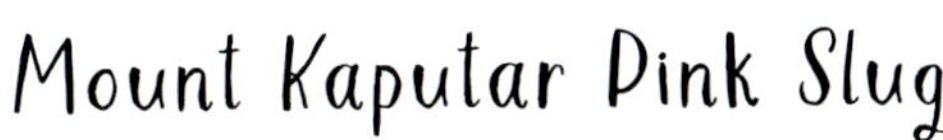

Mount Kaputar Pink Slug

(Triboniophorus aff. graeffei)

These huge (20 cm long!) neon-pink slugs are only found on an extinct volcano in New South Wales. Their bright colour provides camouflage among the fallen red eucalyptus leaves.

Starfish Fungus

(Aseroe rubra)

This stinky fungus grows on mulch and attracts flies with its stench, which smells like rotting meat.

Sturt's Desert Pea

(Swainsona formosa)

The floral state emblem of South Australia, these striking plants were named after explorer Captain Charles Sturt.

Flame Robin

(Petroica phoenicea)

To find food, the Flame Robin waits on low perches, ready to pounce on small bugs.

Mottlecah

(Eucalyptus macrocarpa)

Mottlecah flowers grow up to 10 cm. They are the largest of any eucalypt and attract bees, bugs and birds.

Quandong

(Santalum acuminatum)

Also known as a Native Peach. Not surprisingly with a name like that, Quandong is a tasty bush fruit!

Red Kangaroo

(Osphranter rufus)

The Red Kangaroo is the largest of all land-based mammals in Australia.

BROWN + ORANGE

PURNULULU NATIONAL PARK

The lands of the Jaru and Gija people.

The Purnululu National Park in north-western Australia is a World Heritage Site that extends over 2,400 square kilometres – larger than the Australian Capital Territory! In the park is the Bungle Bungle Range – towers of rock that are shaped like beehives, a result of wind and rainfall over the past 360 million years. The towers are coloured in orange and brown bands.

Orange and brown are colours from the earth – rock, sand, dirt and mud. Many Australian mammals are brown, from the Dingo *(Canis lupus dingo)* to the Rufous Hare-Wallaby *(Lagorchestes hirsutus)*. Orange can be spotted in mountain wildflowers, all the way to the sea! In art, orange is often used to represent light. I use brown to bring an earthy warmth and tone to paintings. Where can you see these colours in your world?

Biscuit Sea Star

(Tosia australis)

Hundreds of small feet on the underside of this sea star leave behind tiny footprints! The Biscuit Sea Star senses sunlight through tiny spots on its arms.

Orange Chat

(Epthianura aurifrons)

This songbird lives in the desert and rarely drinks water. If the parent bird senses danger, it will fake an injury to distract the predator from its young!

Frilled Lizard

(Chlamydosaurus kingii)

Stretching up to 90 cm, this large lizard can run on its two back legs. Its frill raises when it is scared or angry.

Numbat

(Myrmecobius fasciatus)

Numbats shelter in burrows or hollow logs, emerging to hunt termites. They are the animal state emblem for Western Australia.

Platypus

(Ornithorhynchus anatinus)

This unique egg-laying mammal is covered in waterproof fur, which insulates to keep them toasty warm.

Jewel Beetle

(Julodimorpha bakewelli)

This glossy, large beetle is part of the Jewel Beetle family (along with 1,200 species in Australia).

Thorny Devil

(Moloch horridus)

The Thorny Devil's colours change over the day as the desert heats, shifting from browns and oranges to yellows.

Beech Orange *(Cyttaria gunnii)*

This edible fungus grows from Myrtle Beech trees and looks a little like a bunch of orange grapes.

Dingo *(Canis lupus dingo)*

Dingoes have flexible shoulder joints and can rotate their wrists – enough to open doors!

Lumholtz's Tree-Kangaroo

(Dendrolagus lumholtzi)

Tree-kangaroos are the only arboreal macropods, making them the only tree-dwelling marsupials.

Mountain Frog

(Philoria kundagungan)

This endangered species lives in wet forests and near rivers. These tiny frogs only grow up to 3 cm.

Copper Jewel Butterfly

(Hypochrysops apelles)

Like many butterflies, Copper Jewel larvae are kindly helped by ants, who guard them and remove parasites.

Rufous Hare-Wallaby/ Mala

(Lagorchestes hirsutus)

These highly endangered small macropods make underground burrows with spinifex roofs.

Tawny Frogmouth

(Podargus strigoides)

These owl-like birds form partnerships for life and build nests together, taking turns to supply food for their babies.

Christmas Beetle

(Anoplognathus pallidicollis)

These glossy nocturnal beetles eat eucalyptus leaves for their midnight feasts.

Acorn Banksia

(Banksia prionotes)

Growing in the sandy soils of Western Australia, this plant is pollinated by honeyeaters. It provides food and protection for many types of birds and insects.

Southern Hairy-Nosed Wombat

(Lasiorhinus latifrons)

The state animal of South Australia is very friendly – it shares its burrow home with up to ten others!

Bronze Orange Bug

(Musgraveia sulciventris)

Large and slow moving (they stay on the same spot for a few days!), the Bronze Orange Bug produces a stinky liquid when threatened.

Leichhardt's Grasshopper

(Petasida ephippigera)

A very rare grasshopper found in parts of the Northern Territory. It is a very fussy eater!

Honey Possum

(Tarsipes rostratus)

Often mistaken for mice, they feed on the nectar of flowering plants with their long tongues.

Boab *(Adansonia gregorii)*

This useful tree has been highly valued by First Nations Australians. Most parts of it are edible, and it can be used for medicines or to store water.

Orange Leaf-Nosed Bat

(Rhinonicteris aurantia)

This small bat is an insectivore! It likes to live in a big group in warm, humid caves.

Buff-Breasted Paradise Kingfisher

(Tanysiptera sylvia)

These birds make nests in termite mounds to create a warm, safe space to lay their eggs.

Australian Fur Seal

(Arctocephalus pusillus doriferus)

Mother seals feeding at sea can find their pups onshore by listening for their unique call.

Flame Pea

(Chorizema cordatum)

Found in south-western parts of Western Australia, this striking plant is also known as Heart-Leaf Flame Pea or 'Kaly' in the Noongar language.

Australian Painted Lady

(Vanessa kershawi)

This common butterfly is found in urban areas and migrates over huge distances in big groups.

Superb Lyrebird

(Menura novaehollandiae)

This striking, large songbird is an incredible mimic of other birds and forest sounds.

YELLOW

MOUNT KOSCIUSZKO (KUNAMA NAMADGI)

The lands of the Walgalu and Ngarigo people.

Mount Kosciuszko in New South Wales is Australia's highest peak, rising to 2,228 metres above sea level. During spring, the mountain is covered in wildflowers such as Billy Buttons (*Craspedia variabilis*) and Anemone Buttercups *(Ranunculus anemoneus)*, as well as the migrating Bogong Moths (*Agrotis infusa*), which travel for hundreds of kilometres and stay to aestivate – a kind of summer hibernation.

Yellow – the happy and warming colour of sun, sand and summer – can be found all across Australia. Bright yellow can be seen on many flowers, like our national floral emblem, the Golden Wattle (*Acacia pycnantha*). Farms grow fields of yellow canola and heavy bunches of ripening bananas. Yellow can also be spotted on animals, from the shy Kakarratul or Northern Marsupial Mole (*Notoryctes caurinus*) underground all the way to the golden streak of a Yellow-Bellied Glider *(Petaurus australis)* at the top of tall trees. Yellow can be found in art throughout the centuries, all the way back to ancient cave paintings and buried gold-laced sculptures. I love painting with yellow to give a sense of warmth, optimism and light.

Spotted Pardalote

(Pardalotus punctatus)

A tiny bird that forages for insects up very high – it is usually recognised by its call rather than being seen!

Golden-Striped Butterfly Fish

(Chaetodon aureofasciatus)

This fish can sometimes be found near freshwater river mouths, although it usually likes coastal reefs as it dines on corals.

Northern Marsupial Mole/ Kakarratul

(Notoryctes caurinus)

This elusive mole is found underground in the sand dunes of the desert in central Australia.

Golden Sun Moth

(Synemon plana)

The larva lives underground for years, eventually digging to the surface to grow into a moth that lives up to four days.

Crucifix Toad

(Notaden bennettii)

With a distinct cross on their backs, they are also known as Holy Cross Frogs. Their bright colours warn off predators.

Yellow Chat

(Epthianura crocea)

Small birds usually struggle in the heat, but the clever Yellow Chat has a brush-tipped tongue that helps it collect small pockets of water.

Murnong/ Yam Daisy

(Microseris lanceolata)

An alpine herb with sweet-tasting roots, this plant has been a popular and important bush food for some First Nations Australians.

Macleay's Grass Yellow

(Eurema herla)

These tiny, eye-catching butterflies are found over much of the north and east of Australia.

Sulphur-Crested Cockatoo

(Cacatua galerita)

A very smart bird that can live up to a century! Often spotted in Australian cities, hanging out in gregarious groups and screeching loudly.

Yellow-Footed Rock-Wallaby

(Petrogale xanthopus)

These wallabies live in rough terrain and rocky outcrops and forage for grasses and shrubs.

Yellow-Tailed Black Cockatoo

(Zanda funerea)

These large cockatoos are found in the south-east of Australia. They are rather particular about their homes and like to nest in ancient trees.

Golden Bowerbird

(Prionodura newtoniana)

This bird lives in rainforest mountains in north-eastern Queensland and mainly eats tropical fruits and occasionally insects.

Olive-Backed Sunbird

(Cinnyris jugularis)

Found in Queensland, these sunbirds delicately hover while plucking spiders from their webs. The males have iridescent blue chests.

Southern Corroboree Frog

(Pseudophryne corroboree)

Unlike every other poisonous frog, these tiny endangered frogs create their own poison rather than getting it from food sources.

Billy Button

(Craspedia variabilis)

These tall plants with fluffy-looking flower heads (also known as 'woollyheads') grow all over Australia except the Northern Territory.

Wattle

(Acacia sp)

There are around 1,000 species of *Acacia* in Australia and they are all celebrated on National Wattle Day on the 1st of September every year.

Australian Emperor

(Hemianax papuensis)

The female dragonflies lay their eggs underwater while males defend them through air battles!

Pale-Yellow Robin

(Tregellasia capito)

Found in wet forests, these birds build cup-shaped nests to keep their young safe. If a predator approaches, one parent will fake an injury to lure them away!

Leafy Seadragon

(Phycodurus eques)

The marine state emblem of South Australia, these fish resemble seaweed with their camouflaged coverings.

Regent Bowerbird

(Sericulus chrysocephalus)

While the females are a more subdued olive, the spectacular yellow colour is seen on the males. Their eyes even become yellow in their second year!

Yellow-Billed Kingfisher

(Syma torotoro)

These rainforest-dwelling kingfishers usually nest in abandoned termite nests found in trees. They like to sit up high, waiting to pounce on their next meal.

Desert Scorpion

(Urodacus yaschenkoi)

Desert Scorpions can be yellow, red or brown, depending on where they live. They build corkscrew-shaped burrows, which helps keep a stable temperature under the desert's scorching hot ground.

Shortsnout Spikefish

(Triacanthodes ethiops)

This spikefish grows up to 8.5 cm long and is found in deep waters up to 458 m below the surface.

Red-Banded Jezebel/ Union Jack

(Delias mysis)

The fuzzy caterpillars feed on the leaves of mistletoes before growing into beautiful butterflies.

Yellow-Bellied Glider

(Petaurus australis)

Also known as the Fluffy Glider, this possum is around the size of a rabbit and can jump and glide over 100 m.

TARRA-BULGA NATIONAL PARK

The lands of the Gunaikurnai people, Brataualung Country.

This cool, temperate rainforest in Gippsland, Victoria is home to Mountain Ash *(Eucalyptus regnans)* – one of the tallest flowering plants in the world. You'll also find Tree Ferns *(Cyatheales)*, Southern Sassafras *(Atherosperma moschatum)* and Myrtle Beeches *(Nothofagus cunninghamii)*.

Green is the colour of life, found in many plants because of chlorophyll – the pigment that helps plants create their own food. Australian rainforests are luminous with painterly splashes of greens in many different shades. Green is also found on many native animals, often to camouflage in this verdant environment. Sometimes, green helps animals stand out! The Cairns Birdwing Butterfly *(Ornithoptera euphorion)* gleams like a jewel in the forest. Green is a secondary colour in art, and brings me a feeling of calmness when I paint with it. How does it make you feel?

GREEN

Rainbow Bee-Eater

(Merops ornatus)

After catching a bee or wasp, these birds rub it against a perch to remove its sting before eating it!

Green Moon Wrasse

(Thalassoma lutescens)

This brightly coloured fish can change sex from female to male! It lives in coral reefs, usually in groups, and changes colour as it grows.

Cairns Birdwing

(Ornithoptera euphorion)

The female has a giant wingspan of up to 15 cm, making it Australia's largest butterfly.

Night Parrot

(Pezoporus occidentalis)

Once presumed extinct, this elusive and endangered bird has been spotted a handful of times in recent years (and heard a little more often).

Leafy Greenhood

(Pterostylis cucullata)

This low-light orchid flowers from August to October with a single flower emerging from a 'rosette' of leaves.

Green Tree Ant

(Oecophylla smaragdina)

This ant weaves leaves with larvae silk to build balloon-shaped nests in trees. Several nests can be in one tree, all ruled by one queen ant.

Freshwater Crocodile

(Crocodylus johnstoni)

A shy croc found in freshwater creeks and billabongs at the top of Australia. When they're ready to hatch, the baby crocs will call to their mums from inside their eggs.

Green Lacewing

(Mallada signatus)

Helpful in the garden as they eat other bugs, these lacewings have eyes that appear gold and metallic.

Green Anemone

(Cnidopus verater)

Found in southern Australia, they live in deep rock pools, awaiting food that gets washed in with the tide.

Soft Tree Fern

(Dicksonia antarctica)

With a trunk made from decaying leaves, this fern only grows a few centimetres a year but can eventually grow to 15 m tall! It thrives in wet environments.

Green Ringtail Possum

(Pseudochirops archeri)

These large tree-dwelling possums have a green tint to their fur, which helps them camouflage. They exclusively eat leaves.

Common Tree Snake

(Dendrelaphis punctulatus)

Its scales are made from keratin, the same thing that makes up our hair and fingernails!

Greengrocer Cicada

(Cyclochila australasiae)

One of the loudest insects in the world!

Fan Palm

(Licuala ramsayi)

These palms slowly grow to up to 20 m tall with huge 2 m-wide umbrella-like round leaves.

Jewel Beetle

(Stigmodera gratiosa)

This species of Jewel Beetle is found in Western Australia and feeds on wildflowers.

Green Jumping Spider

(Mopsus mormon)

One of the biggest jumping spiders in Australia, they hunt during the daytime by jumping onto their prey. The spiders' nests are built on curved leaves.

Wollemi Pine

(Wollemia nobilis)

The Wollemi Pine is one of the oldest and rarest plants in the world. It was thought to be extinct until a small group were found growing in a canyon in New South Wales.

Australian Ringneck

(Barnardius zonarius)

There are several subspecies of this parrot, but all are mainly green with a ringed neck and grow to around 30 cm. Australian Ringnecks nest in hollow trees and love to eat fruits and nuts.

Green Tree Python

(Morelia viridis)

Grows to 2 m on a diet of small mammals, skinks and lizards. GULP! Baby Green Tree Pythons are bright yellow.

Ghost Fungus

(Omphalotus nidiformis)

Found on dead or dying trees, they appear ghostly white during the day, but at night their bioluminescence turns them a glowing green. Poisonous to eat!

Budgerigar

(Melopsittacus undulatus)

These well-known pets are found across the drier parts of Australia and in huge flocks after rain. Their name is derived from 'Betcherrygah', a Gamilaraay word.

Green Catbird

(Ailuroedus crassirostris)

This bird's curious name comes from its distinctive call, which sounds like a cat meowing.

Macleay's Swallowtail

(Graphium macleayanus)

Green caterpillars hatch from round green eggs and transform into green-and-black butterflies. The 'tail' is a fork on each hindwing.

Gulf Snapping Turtle

(Elseya oneiros)

Although these freshwater turtles are brown, they often look green from the moss that grows on their shell like a little garden island!

Silvereye

(Zosterops lateralis)

The Silvereye's neat nests are made with fine vegetation and bound with delicate spiderwebs.

Magnificent Tree Frog

(Litoria splendida)

These nocturnal frogs hide in caves and rock crevices in the day. Found in the Northern Territory and Western Australia.

Bird's Nest Fern

(Asplenium australasicum)

These ferns have such short roots that they can grow on rocks or trees! They form a nest shape with a rosette of fronds.

THE GREAT BARRIER REEF

The land and sea Country of more than 70 Traditional Owner groups.

The Great Barrier Reef is bigger than Victoria and Tasmania combined, making up over ten per cent of the world's reef ecosystems. It is so big it can be seen from space! The Reef is home for thousands of marine animals, corals and other sea plants, and its beaches are important breeding grounds for many birds and Sea Turtles *(Chelonioidea).*

While blue might be the dominant colour in big landscapes – like the ocean, mountains and sky – it is rarely found on plants and animals. Blue is found in less than ten per cent of the world's flowers. And while some animal skin appears blue, no furry animals are coloured blue! (Curiously, the fur of the Platypus *(Ornithorhynchus anatinus)* glows blue and green under UV light – it's quite a phenomenon!) In art, blue can feel tranquil, reflective and even melancholy – so many emotions and so many pigments, from ultramarine to turquoise. Let's dive deeper into the blues ...

BLUE

Bright Oakblue Butterfly

(Arhopala madytus)

These beautiful small butterflies have a brown underside and vivid blue top with a black border.

Australian Bluefish

(Girella cyanea)

A species of sea chub, the Australian Bluefish can grow over 70 cm. They mainly eat at dawn and dusk on a diet of seaweed, crustaceans, smaller fish, worms and molluscs.

Southern Blue-Ringed Octopus

(Hapalochlaena maculosa)

These lethal creatures blow streams of venom to snare unsuspecting prey.

Blue-Bellied Black Snake

(Pseudechis guttatus)

A shiny bluish-black snake with a blue underside. Although venomous, it is a shy snake that will only strike when threatened.

Southern Cassowary

(Casuarius casuarius)

These impressive birds are the largest of the cassowaries and the third-largest birds on Earth.

Splendid Fairywren

(Malurus splendens)

These tiny birds truly deserve the title of 'splendid'! Their electric blue shades shimmer from their semi-arid woodland homes across much of Australia.

Pygmy Blue Whale

(Balaenoptera musculus brevicauda)

While this beauty can grow to 24 m, it is smaller than its relatives! Pygmy Blue Whales in the south-east Indian Ocean migrate up along the Western Australian coast to breeding zones thought to be in Indonesia.

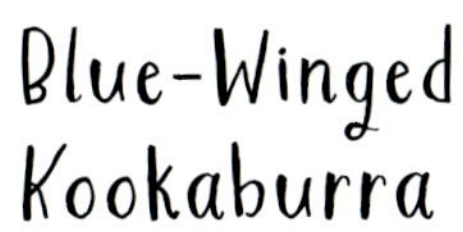

Blue-Winged Kookaburra

(Dacelo leachii)

Their call has been described as a cackle or a bark. They're also known for having a square head and long beak.

Christmas Island Blue Crab

(Tuerkayana celeste)

These special crabs are only found at one place on Earth – Christmas Island. They live in muddy holes near fresh water.

Blue Devil

(Eryngium ovinum)

Found in woodlands, this hardy perennial herb flowers in summer with metallic-blue spiky stems.

Bluebottle

(Physalia physalis)

Bluebottles are actually made up of four 'zooids' (individual animals that are part of a whole) that rely on each other to live.

Tasmanian Blue Gum

(Eucalyptus globulus)

It's called a Blue Gum because of the blueish-green leaves of younger trees, which eventually darken to green.

Azure Kingfisher

(Ceyx azureus)

From their riverside perches, they keep an eye on platypuses to catch any leftovers.

Ulysses Butterfly

(Papilio ulysses)

With a big wingspan of 10 cm, these butterflies are electric blue on top but brown underneath to help blend into their environment.

Western Blue-Tongued Skink

(Tiliqua occipitalis)

Nicknamed 'Bluey', these skinks are shy – but their blue tongue is a warning to potential enemies!

Blue Lady Orchid

(Thelymitra crinita)

Up to 15 flowers emerge from a stem, ranging from pale to dark blue. It's found in coastal forests of Western Australia.

Peacock Spider

(Maratus volans)

A kind of jumping spider known to be able to see the UV-range and every colour of the rainbow! This keen eyesight helps them track and pounce tiny prey.

Little Blue Periwinkle

(Austrolittorina unifasciata)

These small sea snails with pale blue shells are found in the 'splash zone' (where waves or tides come and go) and feed on lichen and algae.

Eastern Blue Groper

(Achoerodus viridis)

A kind of wrasse (not a groper!) and the fish emblem of New South Wales.

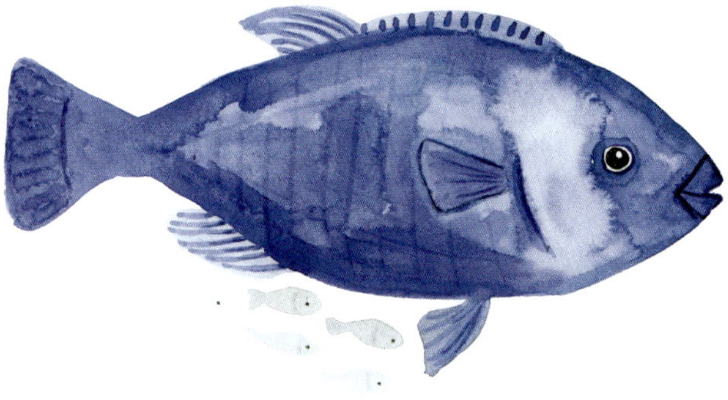

Little Penguin

(Eudyptula minor)

The smallest of penguins, weighing a tiny 1.5 kg. Their blue plumage camouflages them in water, with younger Little Penguins having an even bluer hue.

Blue Pincushion

(Brunonia australis)

This herb grows over much of Australia and is recognised for its cluster of bright blue flowers forming a tight round ball.

Soldier Crab

(Mictyris longicarpus)

Soldier crabs gather into large 'armies' when tides recede, before digging individual corkscrew-like burrows and disappearing underground.

Dollarbird

(Eurystomus orientalis)

Dollarbirds feed on flying insects, capturing them with acrobatic aerial skill!

Smooth Marron

(Cherax cainii)

Can be found in many different shades, including a dazzling electric blue. Found in Western Australia and more recently as aquarium pets across the world.

Satin Bowerbird

(Ptilonorhynchus violaceus)

Well-known for their amazing decorating skills – a male bird will bring all sorts of blue decorations to his bower, like seedpods, feathers and bottle tops!

Blue-Faced Honeyeater

(Entomyzon cyanotis)

This honeyeater is known as the 'banana bird' in tropical areas because it loves eating banana fruit and flowers.

VIOLET + PURPLE

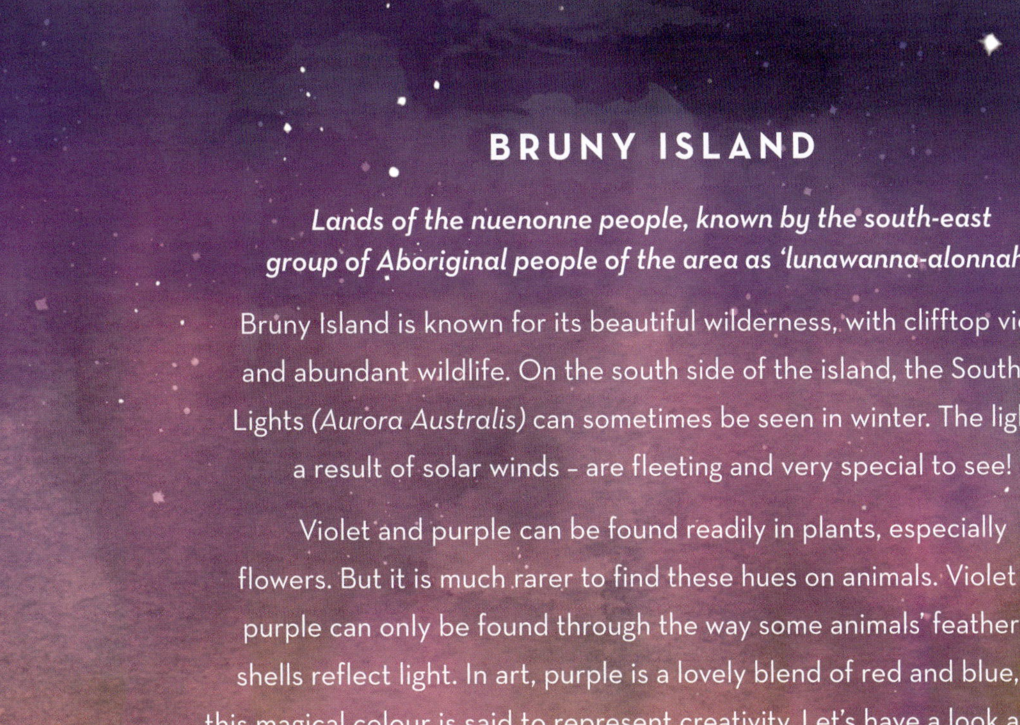

BRUNY ISLAND

Lands of the nuenonne people, known by the south-east group of Aboriginal people of the area as 'lunawanna-alonnah'.

Bruny Island is known for its beautiful wilderness, with clifftop views and abundant wildlife. On the south side of the island, the Southern Lights *(Aurora Australis)* can sometimes be seen in winter. The lights – a result of solar winds – are fleeting and very special to see!

Violet and purple can be found readily in plants, especially flowers. But it is much rarer to find these hues on animals. Violet and purple can only be found through the way some animals' feathers or shells reflect light. In art, purple is a lovely blend of red and blue, and this magical colour is said to represent creativity. Let's have a look at these magical colours and where we might find them in the world around us.

Purple Sea Urchin

(Heliocidaris erythrogramma)

One of the most common species of sea urchin in southern Australian waters. They eat algae and grow to around 11 cm.

Purple-Necked Rock Wallaby

(Petrogale purpureicollis)

It isn't fully understood what creates the soft purple sheen on the necks of these wallabies, but the pigment is darker on males than females.

Jewel Beetle

(Castiarina klugii)

Found in New South Wales and Victoria, this jewel beetle shimmers with deep blues and rich purples (depending on the light).

Chocolate Lily

(Arthropodium strictum)

This chocolate-scented bush flower has edible tubers that can be eaten raw or cooked.

Carpet Sea Star

(Patiriella calcar)

Grows to 10 cm in rocky pools around Australia. It slowly walks on its tube feet, gathering food such as algae and mussels.

Common Dampiera

(Dampiera linearis)

Found in south-west Western Australia, these vivid flowers can withstand bushfires and regrow quickly.

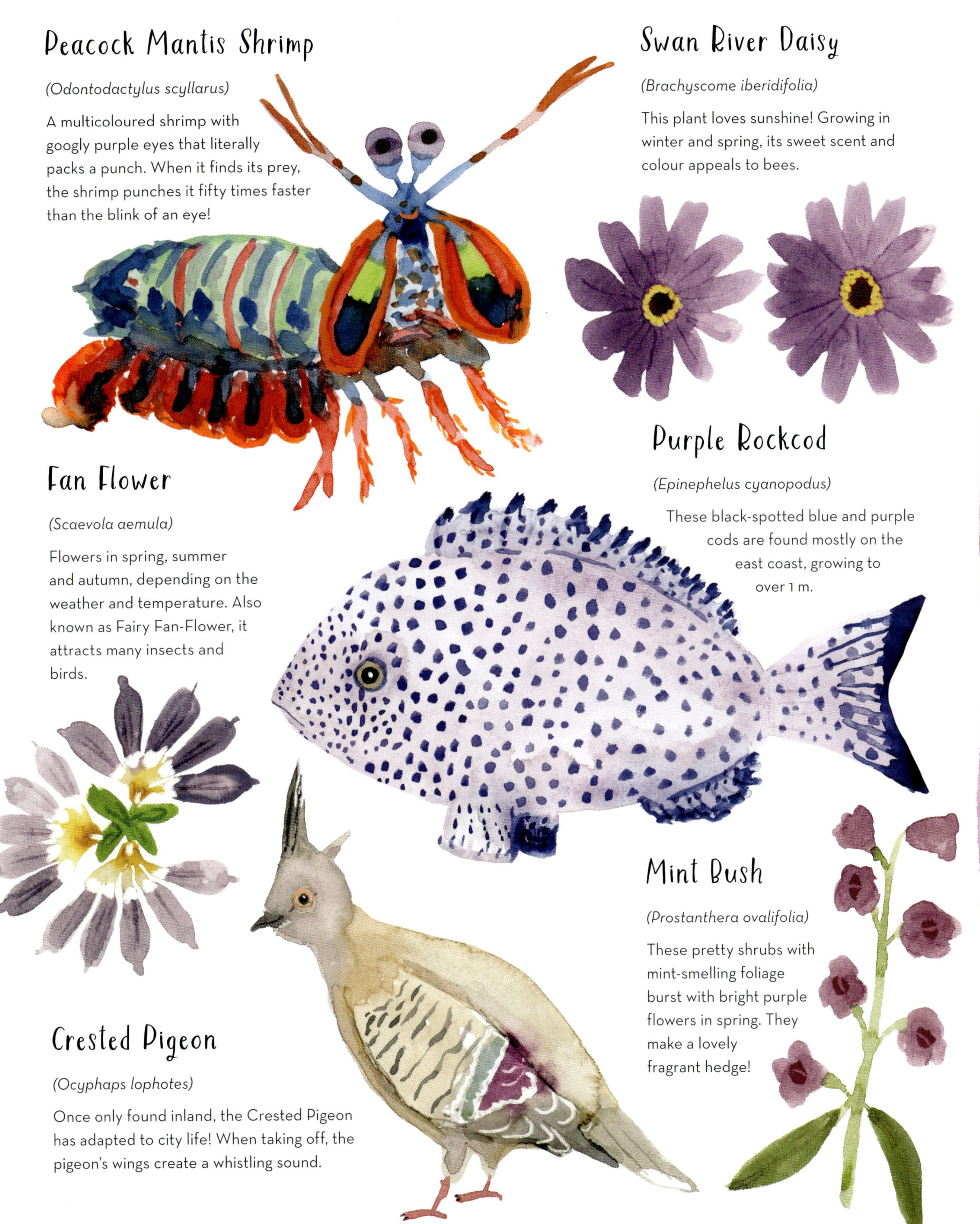

Peacock Mantis Shrimp

(Odontodactylus scyllarus)

A multicoloured shrimp with googly purple eyes that literally packs a punch. When it finds its prey, the shrimp punches it fifty times faster than the blink of an eye!

Swan River Daisy

(Brachyscome iberidifolia)

This plant loves sunshine! Growing in winter and spring, its sweet scent and colour appeals to bees.

Purple Rockcod

(Epinephelus cyanopodus)

These black-spotted blue and purple cods are found mostly on the east coast, growing to over 1 m.

Fan Flower

(Scaevola aemula)

Flowers in spring, summer and autumn, depending on the weather and temperature. Also known as Fairy Fan-Flower, it attracts many insects and birds.

Mint Bush

(Prostanthera ovalifolia)

These pretty shrubs with mint-smelling foliage burst with bright purple flowers in spring. They make a lovely fragrant hedge!

Crested Pigeon

(Ocyphaps lophotes)

Once only found inland, the Crested Pigeon has adapted to city life! When taking off, the pigeon's wings create a whistling sound.

Purple Encrusting Sponge

(Haliclona permollis)

Living in rock pools, this is the only sponge that can thrive in full sunlight. It looks like it has tiny craters or volcanos over its surface!

Bathurst Copper Butterfly

(Paralucia spinifera)

Shades of shimmering copper and purple shine from this endangered butterfly's wings when they rest in the sun!

Boobialla *(Myoporum insulare)*

After summer, the Boobialla's white flowers with purple spots are replaced by purple fruit (which makes tasty jams!).

Western Swamphen

(Porphyrio porphyrio)

These excellent swimmers like to eat frogs and duck eggs among other 'snacks' they find along river and lake shores.

Spotted Sun-Orchid

(Thelymitra ixioides)

This orchid bursts with two to ten flowers, speckled in dots on one long thin stem. Pollinated mainly by insects.

Sunset Frog

(Spicospina flammocaerulea)

The Sunset Frog has a spectacular sunset-coloured body with orange to dark purple and black shades. Discovered in 1994, this amphibian lives in a small pocket of south-west Western Australia.

Northern Purple Spotted Gudgeon

(Mogurnda mogurnda)

A freshwater fish found in northern Australia. It swims in streams, billabongs and muddy pools.

Happy Wanderer

(Hardenbergia violacea)

The Happy Wanderer has lots of names – False Sarsaparilla, Purple Coral Pea and Waraburra. This climbing plant cascades in purple flowers.

Purple-Crowned Fairywren

(Malurus coronatus)

Purple-Crowned Fairywren chicks weigh around the same as a pencil. Breeding males and females remain as a dedicated pair and sometimes perform duets!

Dainty Green Tree Frog

(Litoria gracilenta)

An emblem for the City of Brisbane, this green frog has a maroon-purple thigh.

Cudgegong Giant Spiny Crayfish

(Euastacus vesper)

A rare spiny crayfish with blue or violet claws, found in the Cudgegong River in New South Wales.

Violet Snail

(Janthina janthina)

These seafaring snails create a raft from bubbles to float on the ocean surface.

Sea Hare

(Aplysia dactylomela)

These large gliding sea slugs are well-camouflaged and release a toxic purple dye when threatened.

Austral Bluebell

(Wahlenbergia stricta)

The bluebell's roots and flowers can be edible. Its seeds are so tiny they look like a black powder!

BLACK, WHITE + GREY

KATI THANDA (LAKE EYRE)

Lands of the Arabana people.

Australia's biggest inland lake is the continent's lowest point below sea level and glitters with salt crystals when dry. Once every few years, desert rains bring an awe-inspiring abundance of animals and colour to it.

White, black and grey may sound like dull colours (or shades), but they are anything but that in nature! These shades create drama and contrast, which you'll see in huge grey storm clouds, deep, dark caverns and crisp white snowy mountains. These so-called dreary hues can be found on many animals, including the iconic Koala *(Phascolarctos cinereus)* and Tasmanian Devil *(Sarcophilus harrisii)*. In art, black, white and grey are great for adding detail and depth (they can make paintings look more realistic and three-dimensional) as well as adding drama!

Letter-Winged Kite

(Elanus scriptus)

Its name is from the 'letter' marking – an M or a W – seen in black when in flight. Kites hunt at twilight for rodents.

Zebra Snail

(Austrocochlea porcata)

At certain times of the year, the algae the zebra snail eats causes its shell to form a darkened band.

Southern Myotis

(Myotis macropus)

One of only two 'fishing bats'. Fishes by flying over the water's surface and making their catch with their feet.

Silky Snow-Daisy

(Celmisia sericophylla)

Found in the Bogong High Plains in Victoria, this plant has striking flowers and velvety leaves.

Tasmanian Devil

(Sarcophilus harrisii)

The largest carnivorous marsupial with a loud screeching call. A Devil can also climb trees and swim!

Greater Bilby

(Macrotis lagotis)

These vulnerable bilbies spend their days in burrows, emerging at night to feed.

Spiny Rice-Flower

(Pimelea spinescens)

Critically endangered, this small shrub flowers in winter, helping insects eat at this time of year.

Skirt Webcap *(Cortinarius australiensis)*

This large poisonous mushroom umbrellas to the length of a school ruler. It appears in eucalypt forests between April and July.

Australian White Ibis

(Threskiornis molucca)

Found across Australia and increasingly in urban areas, these birds find food where they can, earning their nickname of 'bin chicken'.

Australian Magpie

(Gymnorhina tibicen)

A well-known bird with a musical warble, magpies are spotted over most of Australia.

Lesser Black Whipsnake

(Demansia vestigiata)

A slender, venomous snake found in woodlands in Queensland, the Northern Territory and Western Australia.

Striped Possum

(Dactylopsila trivirgata)

These striking possums have a strong, musty odour and mainly eat insect larvae. These shy tropical dwellers inhabit the northern tip of Queensland.

Mueller's Snow Gentian

(Gentianella muelleriana)

These plants live for several seasons and have pretty white flowers on tall stems.

Koala (*Phascolarctos cinereus*)

There are three subspecies of koala. Smaller and lighter koalas are found in Queensland, while larger, browner types are found further south.

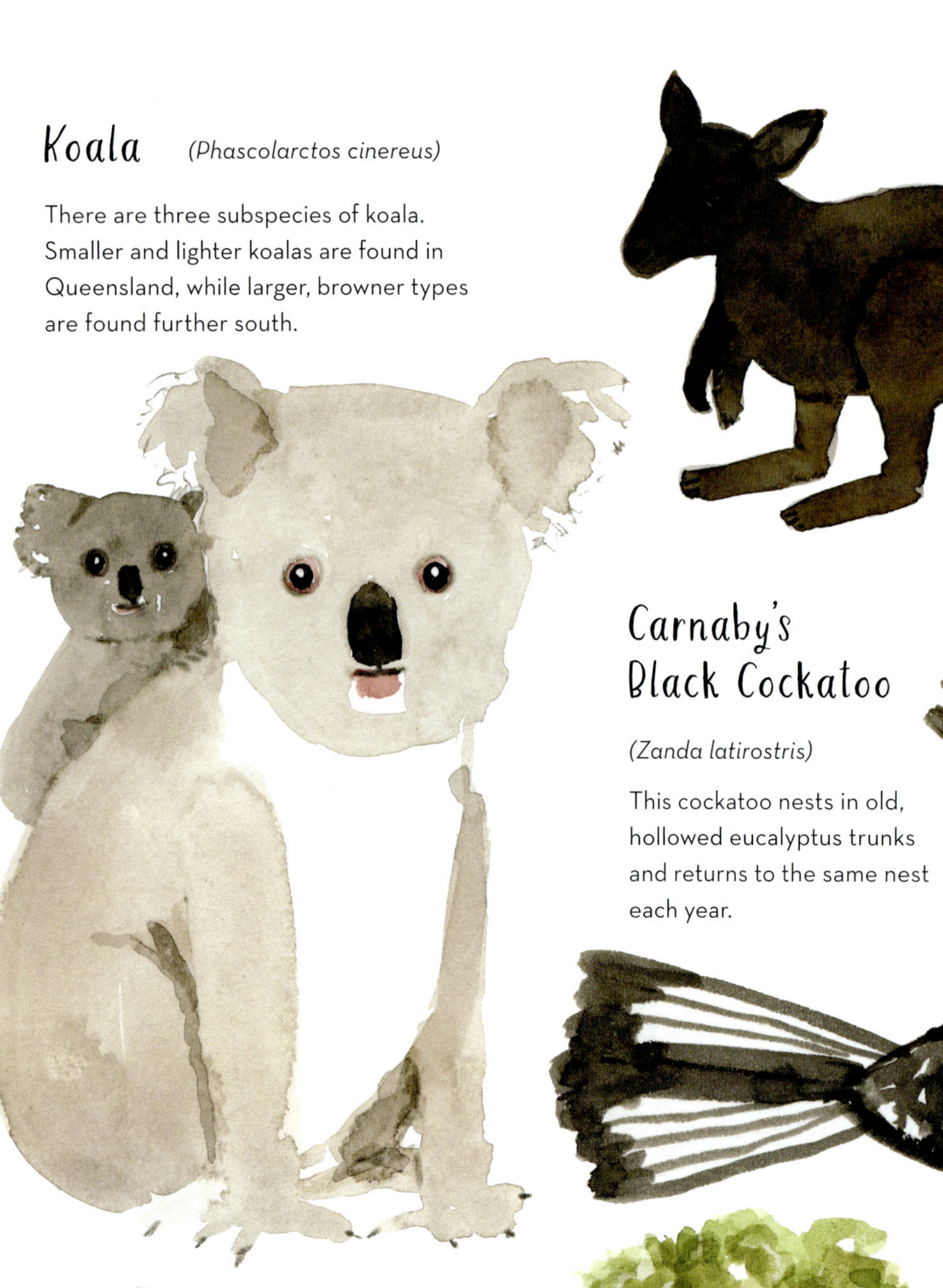

Black Wallaroo

(Osphranter bernardus)

These are the smallest of the wallaroos. Only the males have dark black fur – the females are lighter.

Carnaby's Black Cockatoo

(Zanda latirostris)

This cockatoo nests in old, hollowed eucalyptus trunks and returns to the same nest each year.

Pied Monarch

(Arses kaupi)

The small Pied Monarch is found in coastal Queensland and lives on a diet of flying insects, such as moths and butterflies.

Black Ironbark

(Eucalyptus sideroxylon)

Red, pink, white or yellow flowers bloom from April to December on this striking eucalyptus, also known as Red Ironbark or Mugga Ironbark.

Ghost Gum

(Corymbia aparrerinja)

The Ghost Gum grows in central Australia and has smooth, bright white bark.

Irukandji Jellyfish

(Carukia barnesi)

A small jellyfish with long tentacles, known for its painful sting.

Bandy-Bandy

(Vermicella annulata)

Also known as Hoop Snakes, these venomous snakes are quickly recognised by their unique pattern.

Fairy Tern

(Sternula nereis)

Fairy Terns can dive from five-metres high to catch fish. They live in coastal areas as well as salty and freshwater wetlands.

Banded Stingaree

(Urolophus cruciatus)

Found along the coasts of south-eastern Australia, these stingrays spend the day still under the sand, only emerging for snacks.

Eastern Grass Owl

(Tyto longimembris)

This long-legged owl is also known as Daddy Long-Legs Owl. It nests on the ground and hunts at night, guided by its sharp hearing.

Grey Fantail

(Rhipidura albiscapa)

Constantly on the move, wagging their tails and catching insects with agile acrobatics.

AUTHOR'S NOTE

While researching this book, I was struck by the way in which this country's flora and fauna exist, and how quickly this has changed in more recent times. For more than 60,000 years, Australia's First Peoples have had a strong connection to the sea, land and animals and built a rich knowledge of looking after Country. Some unique species are found in tiny pockets of Australia and nowhere else on Earth! Sadly, some of these plants and animals are currently threatened with extinction.

With such a long history of living in harmony with Country, the expertise of Australia's First Peoples is vital for all Australians to better understand the delicate balance of our natural environment.

There are some wonderful organisations working to support our country in different ways. Here are some groups I like to learn from:

Seed
www.seedmob.org.au

Australian Wildlife Conservancy
www.australianwildlife.org

BirdLife Australia
www.birdlife.org.au

Bush Heritage
www.bushheritage.org.au

A big thank you to the scientists Libby Rumpff, Sarah Legge and John Woinarski for their assistance identifying many of these colourful plants and animals, as well as their vital work as scientists, also working to restore balance in this delicate and unique environment. Thank you to Kristy Lund-White for her incredible design skills piecing together all these artworks like a jigsaw puzzle! Thank you to Davina Bell for being an ideas springboard and getting as excited as me about projects, always. Thank you to Samone Amba and Coral Huckstep for editing the huge wall of text so expertly. Thank you to Tash Besliev for her commitment and care to help the book be the very best it could be. Thank you to Affirm Press for always getting behind my projects with such passion and energy.

First published in Australia in 2023 by Affirm Press,
a Simon & Schuster (Australia) Pty Limited company

This edition published by Affirm Press in 2024
28 Thistlethwaite Street, South Melbourne VIC 3205
Bunurong/Boon Wurrung Country

Affirm Press is located on the unceded land of the Bunurong/Boon Wurrung peoples of the Kulin Nation.
Affirm Press pays respect to their Elders past and present.

New York Amsterdam/Antwerp London Toronto Sydney/Melbourne New Delhi

Visit our website at www.simonandschuster.com.au

10 9 8 7 6 5 4 3 2

A Cataloguing-in-Publication entry for this book is available from the National Library of Australia

9781923135840 (paperback)

Cover and internal design by Kristy Lund-White
Printed and bound in China by RR Donnelley Asia